Edwin Ross Champlin

Heart's Own

Verses

Edwin Ross Champlin

Heart's Own
Verses

ISBN/EAN: 9783744665476

Printed in Europe, USA, Canada, Australia, Japan

Cover: Foto ©Thomas Meinert / pixelio.de

More available books at **www.hansebooks.com**

HEART'S OWN

VERSES

BY

EDWIN R. CHAMPLIN

———

CHICAGO
CHARLES H. KERR & COMPANY
1886

CONTENTS.

Contents.

Out of my heart I send you forth, O tender-
thoughted crew,
And may you find a resting-place in hearts
I never knew.

NOTE.

MOST of the pieces in this book have not been published; those which have been will doubtless be readily recognized by most readers. My aim in bringing these together has been to present a representative collection of my later verse. The fact that the collection contains some pieces of very little consequence should be considered in the light of this reflection. I thank all who have aided me in bringing out the volume, including the J. B. Lippincott Company, who kindly granted the use of " A Lover's Mood," on which they own the copyright.

MEMORIES.

O MUSIC I've heard, I hear you still,—
  I shall hear you again,—
    I shall hear you forever in heaven !

O sweet I have breath'd, I breathe you now,—
  I shall breathe you till death,—
    I shall hold all your fragrance forever !

O skies I have seen, I see you yet,—
  I shall see you again,—
    I shall see you when new sight is given !

O thoughts that were dear, I have you still,—
  I shall have you again,—
    For your music, your breath, and your
      skies depart never !

A LOVER'S MOOD.

O LIPS, be still, and let the heart make speech:
Her lightest thought is far beyond your reach.
And, worldly wisdom, unto faith give sway:
Your brightest light but darkens this dim day.

A place to rest in, tender sense of love,
The heart that seeks still finds,—whate'er ye
    prove,
Lip-speech, earth-lore, that men account so
    wise,—
Still in the dark hears lovers' sweet replies,

All heedless of the distance that divides,
Since in all space the lover's soul abides,
And knows and trusts the heart against its
    own,
As heart by tongue to heart is ne'er made
    known.

Sing, then, thy song, O heart whose beat I
    hear:
She is not far when thought of her is near,

And she must hear thy singing over all
That world-lore saith or foolish lips let fall.

A LOST BOY.

Where is the boy I used to know—
　My oldest comrade, nearest kin—
In the bright lost land of Long Ago,
Where all boys longed, with me, to grow
　To height of men, and the gold to win
　That we count dross in the land I'm in?

A thousand times I've wished I knew,
　Thinking back with sore, sad heart,
Where that dear comrade wandered to.
　He did'nt *die*; what *did* he do,
(I ask), when he and I did part,
　And I came on to this land of art?

I never knew (it seems most strange)
　The time we parted,—what we said;
Only know there's a wondrous change,
　And often wonder where *he* did range,

And question oft if he be dead;—
  For I haven't seen him since I fled

The land where we were one, and went
  Through the common fields with hearts of
      joy,
Nor dreamed of parting, or discontent
  In the long, long days I here have spent,
When I should question for him—lost boy.
  O child! have *you* found all gold alloy ?

I see him yet in that far-off land,
  And he and I in that land are one!
If he never returns, I shall see him stand
  With his fresh bright eye and his fair soft
      hand,
In the long, long past; and when *that* is gone,
  I may see him where all unto each are
      known!

DEFENSE.

WHEN shadows of base thoughts upon me
 steal,
My soul her silvery-gleaming shield uprears,
And every shade darts back to where 'twas
 born,
In that dark world whence all death's shad-
 ows come.
Love is that shield, and heaven, whence it
 came,
Doth reënforce it with its own pure light.
So shall it brighten in the years to be,
No shade of sin shall dare my soul assail.

DYING AT EIGHTY.

JULY 14, 1886.

WHERE art thou now, O Friend
So near thy journey's end?
Hear'st thou through dream the song
Thine ears have waited long?

Seest thou Christ's face and theirs
Who've climbed the heavenly stairs?
Feel'st thou new life and power,
Perpetual youth thy dower?

Or art thou dead to all
Sweet sounds from heaven let fall?
And seest no face or form,
Nor feel'st or cold or warm,
Dead as men seem to those
Who watch their last repose?

Once thou wert strong and glad;
Once thou didst hear and see,
And feel life's good and glee,
And none for thee were sad,
For *all were glad with thee.*

Some went the same strange way
Thou goest; none came back
To tell us if their track
Lay. through the night or day,—

If silence as in sleep
Held them fast-bound awhile,

And then they woke to smile
With those who used to weep,
Now free from pain and guile;— ·

Or if they went to heaven,
And, *conscious of new rest,
In end of all their quest,
Found that for which they'd striven:
Life of and with the blest;

Or if they went to dust,
Voiceless and sightless, reft
Of all man's glory, left
In old Death's hold and trust,
Of Life's dear body cleft.

And now, while thou go'st out
As *they* went, where the shout
Of comrades we ne'er hear,
And only *dream* them near,—
We wonder how and where
Thou farest—here or there.
Yet, though we knew thee well,
We shall not hear thee tell.

Where thou art now, kind heart,

None knoweth but in part;
But on what journey gone,
Well knoweth every one.
Hear thou at length the song
Thine ears have waited long!
See thou Christ's face and theirs
Who've climbed the heavenly stairs!
Feel thou new life and power,
Perpetual youth thy dower!

ON A FRIEND'S RETURN.

O FACE that dims all dreams!
    Time stops to give thee place!
Rare lily of life's streams,—
    Still lives the olden grace;
Still, in thy mouth's bright gleams,
    Still, in thine eyes I trace
    Such love as neither space
    Nor time can e'er efface.

Robed in thine olden guise,
    Lookest thou on me here;

Unchanged in any wise,
  Dead to each vanished year,
'Live to all lover's ties.
  Friends fade and disappear ;
  Still may I hold thee dear,
  Faithful though far or near !

INHERITANCE.

THE space of the greatest of earth
  Doth shrink to a little dark dwelling
Not they but a greater doth keep,
  In spite of their stoutest rebelling.

When I saw them lie down at Death's call,
  Poor tenants that late were proud keepers,
And heard the vast multitudes moan
  At the change that had come to the
    sleepers,

I thought of the word of the Lord,
  And I longed that the living might fear it:
" The meek are the blest," saith the word,
  " For they shall the kingdoms inherit."

LOVE'S FAITHFULNESS.

LOVE hid himself from me so many days,
I felt myself abandoned ; sick at heart
That one I counted true should leave me so,
I thinned, and fevered, and complained, and
      wept;
My world became a dark, wild-rolling cloud,
      presaging storm ;
When, lo! one day dear Jen came up to me,
And turning her bright eyes full up to mine,
And touching her sweet lips against my
      own,—   *
Mine, parched with Love's long absence,
      fain to turn
Back into mold,—gave me a clasp
Of those rich lips, oft-kissed in dear Love's
      day,   [youth.
That brought Love back in all the bloom of
He had not died; nor fled so far away
But that *one word* might bring him back
      to me,—   [days,
But one long kiss, like those in Love's first
Might bring him in the beauty of his youth !

LOSS AND SALVATION.

WHEN the ship went down in the sea,
  One soul drank the sea to his death,
  Because there was none underneath
To hold him up where Life was free,
  And the sea could not rob him of breath.
And musing on his destiny,
  I thought, Never one of Christ's crew
That are beating up Life's troubled sea,
But the Lord will bring with him, saith he,
  When the heavenward journey is through.

WHEN NEED IS GREATEST.

WHEN need is greatest,
  Heaven is nearest.
  O Thou that to the soul appearest,
And its thirst satest
  From thy full fount,
To thee at earliest beam and latest
  I mount—I mount!

A FADED FLOWER.

IF in my heart the love
   I once confessed to you,
   And fancied deep and true,
   Should blossom out anew,
And I its worth should prove,

Would I confess again?
   Ah! Love in youth is blind;
   Bereft of half its mind:
   It *dreams* it loves, to find
At length dream-love is vain.

Some color won its eye,
   Some turn of head or foot:
   A smile, or signal mute
   Of fondness; or pursuit
Congenial; or some sly

Sweet token wrong-construed.
   Love fancies easily;
   And ere a week goes by
   'Twill for its object die;—
Said I not that *I* would?

I thought I loved thee true;
   I *would* have died for thee.
   To-day where thou mayst be
   I do not know: how free
I feel! I love—not you!

The love that in an hour
   Within me blossomed so
   Is dead; how it *did* glow,
   And set its leaves for show!
'Twas but a passion-flower!

'Tis dead; and not again
   Shall I its bloom behold;
   Dead, and gone into mold;
   Like fancies manifold,
That, dying, gave no pain.

And should it bloom anew,
   It would so fragile seem,
   Like as a bloom of dream,
   And not of Love's pure stream,
I'd say *no word* to you!

BARRIERS.

IF fear of death would die,
  And love of truth increase,
Far-off desire come nigh,
  Distrust and anger cease,

How would the soul upmount
  As on an eagle's wings,
Drink from a heavenly fount,
  And sing as seraph sings!

But while we droop with fear,
  And tremble with distrust,
Desire comes never near,
  Against our loves we lust;

We cannot lift our souls
  Beyond these self-built bars:
And ours are earthly goals,
  Who thought to reach the stars!

REUNION.

If all are " here," it little matters:
   Who fought and died have found it well:
The grave nor censures nor yet flatters;—
   And here is heaven, and here is hell.

Who fought and live have grown the wiser;
   They love so well their friends and foes,
They feel alike to giver, miser,
   The sense of debt that each man owes.

Who live or sleep, if all forgiven,
   If here or there, have had life's best:
To meet on earth, or e'en in heaven,
   Would not be joy, would not be rest.

If all are "here," it little matters:
   Who fought and died have found their
     own;
Nor can Death deal, as shot that scatters,
   A blow that leaves a brave alone!

A PRAYER.

O Love that hast no equal, make me meek !
. That with new eyes thine image I may see,
  And know how far thy kindness unto me
Exceeds the love of them that their love
    speak !
Help me to grow in strength, who am so weak,
  By service great or small, as pleaseth thee.
  I care not, now, to stand with royalty,
But where I am, thy pleasure would I seek.

Now to go forward, and look not behind ;
  Now to reach out and lead the wanderer
      back ;
  Now more to heed the light on mine own
      track,
Nor spy for sins whereto I should be blind,
  Would I, O God : but I in vain must seek
  This way or that till thou hast made me
      meek.

AN OLD STORY.

"Good-by, dear," I heard him say
Just before he went away:
Words that, said some earlier year,
With a lover's youthful cheer,
Would have sounded, oh, how sweet !
But to-day, though they repeat
Sense of love as deep as then,
Seem like words of other men
On his partner's ear to fall—
Empty ceremonial !

And I said, with sinking heart,
So our early dreams depart !
Who to hearts can e'er restore
That which, fled, returns no more ?
Who can resurrect a trust
That is buried in the dust ?
Who, when Pride usurps the place
That was meant for Love to grace,
Can receive with olden cheer
From her mate, "Good-by, my dear"?

THE THINGS A LITTLE CHILD
CAN DO.

THE things a little child can do
Are never great and always few;
But those that men grown great pursue
(Remember when your life looks blue)
Are those to whose pursuit they grew
 From doing smallest duties;
And this is what I'd say to you
 I love so well, my beauties:

The faithful doer of little things—
Though it be but winding broken strings–
Shall one day sit by side of kings
(Not kings with crowns and diamond rings—
Kings of *soul*); for the mighty springs
 From the weak, and true pursuing
Of the little work the present brings
 Will fit you for kingly doing.

SILENT TRUST.

In this loud strife, where tongues and swords
    prevail,
  I, who would surely win the victory,
Need not to fear the foes that me asail,
    For, though I seek my armor silently,
      My God doth fight with me.

In that still hour when, life's worst foes
    o'ercome,
  I seek the rest that follows victory;
I shall not fail to find my welcome home,
    Although as silent, then, my lips may be—
      My God will watch for me !

He who, in strife, or in the peace of death,
  Knows who is his, and who his enemy,
Looks at the heart, and never at the breath ;
    And, though I pray, or though I silent be,
      Fights, leads, and rests with me !

A RHYME OF DUTY.

There was never loss so great
  As of sense of debt to all.
  Let the suffering selfist call,—
Lacking thee, meet whatso fate;
  Evil only can befall
  By neglect of due to all.

Singly every man must die,
  Singly live, and singly strive;
  But to all that are alive,
Not to friend or enemy,
  Must he of his treasure give,—
  Help the world, not one, to thrive.

So, alone, is self preserved,—
  Not by toilsome penury:
  Giving out will bring to thee
All thy loving gifts deserved,
  Build thee up in charity,
  Help all men along with thee.

A DAY.

It came in blackness shrouded,
And all my spirit clouded;
And, till its dreaded form went,
It filled my soul with torment!

But when it had ·departed,—
Such glory it imparted;
Such glimpses it revealèd
Of what it had concealèd

Beneath its grim apparel—
I saw that I might bear well
All pain of soul and spirit
Its beauty to inherit !

THE LOST MESSENGER

Where he fell, none know—none *care*;—
He was bearing the banner of love:
And to know that he bore lover's share
Is enough—till we meet him above !

LOVE'S DEATH.

Bow thy head;
Let naught be said;
Not man is dead,
 But Love.

When tears are shed,
Some heart has bled
For one who's fled
 Above;

Its hope is sped:
Uncomforted,
It mourns as dead
 Its Love.

But when Love's dead—
O woful stead!—
Hearts silent tread
 Life's groove;

For no tear shed,
And no word said,

One *more* than dead
 Can prove.

Bow thy head;
Let naught be said;
Not man is dead
 But Love.

A SONG OF GOD'S COMFORT.

WHEN thought of loss brings tears,
 And sorrows grow more sore,
In vision rare appears
 The Lord that I adore :
His wordless peace is nearest,
My thought of Him is dearest,
When earthly lot is drearest,
 And fled the dreams of yore.

And if *thy* youth's hopes fade,
 Thy manhood's vigor wane,
Love flee, and trust's betrayed,
 And life yield 'neath the strain :

Still, when thy case is sorest,
The Lord whom thou adorest,
O soul that vain implorest
    Man's aid, will thee sustain.

TO D. G. R.

Rossetti ! I, who know thee not, but may
  Some day when I can trace to thine abode,
  Would tell thee how like water when the
      road
Is parched that I have followed all the day,—
No brook in sight that might my thirst
      allay,—
  Is that sweet stream that from thy spirit
      flowed.
  Ah ! many a freshened soul to thee has
      owed
The slake of thirst that kept him on his way,
And visions of the heavenly home of Love
  That in thy liquid draughts so bright
      appear.
Thy " Damozel" still leaneth from above ;

Thy "Lost Days" are our own : thy soul
    is near.
The chaste, new beauty of thy verse
    hath grace
To make us long some day to see thy
    face.

A VICTOR'S MESSAGE.

O LIVING men and dying!
    The way to conquer death
Is not by weak defying,
Nor cowardly complying,
    But by a joyful breath,
With all life's colors flying!

THE WANDERER.

I AM not hard to please, although I dis-
    contented be;
A little loving company were all the world
    to me!

A WANDERER'S PRAYER.

WHAT can I do without Thee?
What, but deny and doubt Thee?
O Master! guide me to thy feet;
And make my life with Thine complete.

Teach me Thine own humility!
Mine eyes are blurred; I cannot see
How like the world my soul has grown
Since I have been these years alone.

Give sight, as in Thine earthly days
Thou gav'st it to the outer phase,
And make me, seeing self anew,
To Thee return, to Thee be true.

ATTITUDE.

Teach the teachers; but with humility
Give heed to all;—the least can still teach
    thee!

TO A FELLOW-WORKER.

Spread not thyself; but know the second's
    grace,
  The moment's beauty—aye, the moment's
    power :
  The crown of all perfection's in some
    hour,—
And all the minutes in the century's space
Some great work grew in, hold fore'er their
    place :—
  If their part fell, fall'n were the glorious
    tower !
  Nor count thy gift as small beside another's
    dower :
None ever wrought to purpose in disgrace
  With his own eyes; but men most small,
To the world's sight, have wrought, in modest
    thought,
  So nobly that at length the tongues of all
Have praised them with a praise they never
    sought.
All's thine, O Soul ! time's long;—each
    moment full ;

Work with thy might, and leave no spaces
   dull !

THE RECALL.

COME back to me!
   Oh let me feel thy heart
Close-pressed to mine as in the days of
   wooing !
Stand here by me,
   And know thyself a part
Of all the life I live, and all that I'm pursuing.

All I have lost,
   O Love, since thou wert near,
Then will return, and thou be more than ever!
   Love that's been crossed
      May yet have title clear
To lasting life, and thou and I ne'er sever !

TRANSGRESSION.

What wisdom hath he gained who knows
    the bound,
  And pays it faithful heed, where glee
    should end,
  Allegiance terminate 'twixt friend and
    friend,
Or toil-strife cease,—to leave the spirit
    sound !
Through every hour do sorrow's moans
    resound,
  Repentance and resolve their voices blend,
  Because herein the sons of men offend ;
And hearts are hourly cursed that else were
    crown'd,
  Because to play, or fancied love, or need,
They gave their souls, nor thought of aught
    beside
  Till roused at last to find their only meed
Sea-apples dead,—and loss of soul abide.

So easy is it to transgress the line
Of righteousness, when few indeed decline !

VANISHED LIGHTS.

THEY who've gone out, that once did shine
        on me,
    And in whose sight I gloried more tnan
        sun,
    Cannot their shining have forever done,
Nor I have ceased fore'er their light to see.
Somewhere, when I, like them, no more
        shall be
    To any outward sense of any one
    That still lives on, shall I not in their sun
My spirit bathe,that mourns them ceaselessly?

The love of life, for life's own sake, is strong;
    The love of truth and God grows day by
        day :
But, loving life, and truth, and God, I long
    (Whatever new stars greet me on my way)
For the old lights that left me in the dark,
With but this hope their trackless way to
        mark.

TO A ROSE'S REMAINS.

O SWEET wild rose,
　Thy seeming death
　　Is an immortal memory;—
Thy life outgoes
　To meet the breath
　　Of souls that in all life to be
　　Shall see thee from thy thorn-bush
　　　free,
Where blossom never withereth,
But beauty blows,—
　No thorn beneath,—
　　In endless fields eternally,
And music flows
　With fragrant breath
　　In spirit seas of harmony.

Mourn not that thou thy shape must
　　lose,—
　We, too, must lay our vesture by;—.
Nor grieve if in thy dwelling high
Thou find'st no rose—*there* all sweets
　　fuse—

No beauty for an earthly eye;
Thou shalt be safe from storm and bruise,
And share our immortality!

IN MAY.

WHO cannot be content in crowds of men
Should take him, in the May-days, to the
fields,
And, where the wall shuts out the rasping
wind,
Lie in the sun, and watch the rising earth.
There is a sense of kinship in the soul
With every stone and every solid thing;
And, sheltered by a wall in sunlight lying,
List'ning to far-off birds, that dart o'er fields
New-cut by plows, on to their leafy homes,
And watching mellowing sod and warming
water,
Fills us with cheer, and hope of better days.
While kings are sad, and slaves see only
death,
Thou by the wall art raised to such a height,
The woe of life's unfelt, its joy alone appears.

CRITERIA.

To every one this mandate comes at last :
  Choose thou the standard thou wouldst
    be judged by !
  And every one *does* choose, for, though we
    fly
All others' sight, we cannot fly him past
Who speaks and earth dissolves or else stands
    fast ;
  Nor,—free as air to choose or low or high,—
  Can any drown or silence that breast-cry ;
Then, having chosen, each will often cast
Such censure on his soul for his base choice,
  Will so reproach him that he could be proud
    To be thus judged e'en by the low and
    vain,
That, should he dare to give his thought a
    voice,
  Both low and high would own their guilt
    avow'd,
    And long to choose (as choose they
    might !) again.

WAITING FOR LOVE.

I'll wait for thee, O love unseen,
  Of whom I've dreamed, for whom I've
    planned,
Let whatso distance intervene
Thy darling soul and mine between;
  Love's language we can understand—
  Love's wire extends from land to land.

I know that thou wilt come to me
  When tides are fair and skies are bright;
And, thinking of the days to be,
My heart, once weak with misery,
  Grows strong with rapturous delight.
  Come,—early, late,—O welcome sight!

AFTER THE VANISHING.

My life, that late did glitter like a star
    Gold-red and full,
  In Love's blue firmament,
Since she that lit it so hath gone so far,
    Lies shrunk and dull,
  Its spirit well-nigh spent!

O Heart of Light, that givest *all* their glow,—
    Maker of skies
  And all the stars that shine!
In the new heavens shall not that spirit
    show,—
    Lit by those eyes,
  Shall not th' old joy be mine?

ON A GLIMPSE.

(FROM MY WINDOW IN MAY.)

O SHINING grass and shining sky,
Together gleam !—for those who die
Some other grass and sky may shine,
But those who grieve and those who pine
Need look on ye when graves are green,
To know life's road is lined with sheen !

Shine on, to show incessantly
Some token of the glow to be !
Shine, that the joy that liveth yet
In men may overcome regret,
And that all hearts may know how fair
The world that lies beyond despair !

A PRISONER.

In Poverty's dark cell I sit,
 But God's rich skies above me shine,
 And beams my face with joy divine,
For with his love my heart is lit.

Am I not king, to him who owns
 The little kingdoms of the earth?
 A loving heart hath greater worth
Than any king's dominions!

In Poverty's dark cell I sit,
 And gaze upon the heavenly faces
 That bid me to those luminous spaces
Through which, at length, my soul shall
  flit.

"IN THE HOLLOW OF THY HAND."

THE living or the dead
　　Who rest, O God, in Thee,
Need not a castle bed
　　Or gates' security :

Guests of the King, indeed !
　　All others are but slaves,
Wear they the monarch's weed,
　　Or lie in guarded graves.

THE GIFT OF YEARS.

THE Years that came and left me, one by one,
　　Brought me a gift that I may keep forever;
The sense that Time's a stream that's never
　　　　run,
　　That Love's the greatest force beneath the
　　　　sun,
And God from Man not God himself can
　　　　sever.

REMEMBERED.

I CANNOT hear the wind's voice sigh,
  But through it all I hear her sighing;
I cannot watch the sunshine lie
  On dew'd green fields, but her smile's
    vying
In my young heart; I cannot feel
  The south-wind's kiss, but still all through
    me
Runs that sweet thrill I used to feel
  Whenever she came nearest to me !
I cannot smell the sweetest rose
  June brings as gentle Summer's suitor,
But all around her being glows,
  And perfume sheds than rose-breath
    sweeter !

She is not dead; she cannot die!
  God doth in fairest mansions keep her;
And while she lives in memory,
  I will not mourn, I cannot weep her!

IF THOU SHUTTEST THINE EAR.

If thou shuttest thine ear
  To the meaningless din
Of the world, thou canst hear
  A fit song to join in
From Eternity clear;—
  A song of his word
That is sung day and night,
  And by spirit-ear heard
From the Infinite Height:
  "BE STRONG IN THE LORD,
AND THE POW'R OF HIS MIGHT!"

A MOTTO.

WHOEVER you are, and whatever you do,
Here's a good motto for you to pursue :
    In the dark,
      In the light,
    In the peace,
      In the fight,
Merry and true—Merry and true!

CONFIDENCE.

I WILL not fear what Love may do.
  Fill not my mind with thoughts of fear!
  Why *should* I fear, when I can hear:
" Heart's own is true! Heart's own is true"?

Some written word may mystify,
  Or lack in gentleness of sound ;
But I can trust that charity
  Which never gives or takes a wound.

And so I banish thought of fear,
  And wait for Love's expression new :
The old words dear that greet my ear:
  " Heart's own is true! Heart's own is
    true!"

GROWTH.

THE river that I knew, a child,
  How wide and deep its waters seemed!
To-day I saw the stream, and smiled!
  Had air absorbed it, or I dreamed?

The house that was my childhood home,
  How high its roof-tree used to be;
But now how shrunken seems its dome,
  How short the stairs once climbed by me.

So shrink the things of sense and time,
  While those of life eternal grow;
The things we dreamed not of, sublime,
  Replacing things we used to know.

WORDSWORTH.

WORDSWORTH, who drank of truth and love
　As men drink water, from the heavenly
　　springs ;
Who, while he walk'd the earth, with head
　above
　Sang heaven-sweet of earth's unhonored
　　things ;
And showed, as none had ever shown before,
　That God and man are one, though far
　　apart,—
Wordsworth still points man upward as of
　yore,
　And leads the way with pure and patient
　　heart !

HEARING.

" Take heed how ye hear."

In silence, and apart from other men,
   When God's great voice some waiting soul
      had heard,
   Were writ those words of might that so
      have stirred
The hearts they touched that they have lived
      since then!
What heed give such to word of tongue or pen
   Spoke in God's name, whene'er the world
      has erred,
   Or he some trying duty has conferred,
And many hear not—listening unto men!

In silence still, and from all souls apart,
   Must thou attend to hear his message great,
Or not to thee will God the charge impart
   Whereby to wake the sleeping church or
      state:
Who dimly hears the message of his Lord
Can never be entrusted with that word.

SHELTER.

To feel, when the winds are wild, and full of
  keen drawn swords,
The shield of a wayside house, or a great
  high fence, or a wall,—
Ah, that is joy, fair friend, who sittest in
  parlors warm,
And knowest but what men tell of the hard-
  ship of wind and storm:—
Joy above all thy feasts, thy greetings of
  fondest friends,—
Above (if I read aright the writing in
  mine own heart)
Thy dearest *positive* joy; for, negative
  though it be,
'Tis a symbol of other joy, so strong and
  comforting,
That my heart would be cold as the winds,
  and this shelter a blank to me,
If God's great love should depart!

A THOUGHT AFTER A PETITION.

WHAT though we hear no voice
      In answer to our prayer?
      Something subdues despair,
   Something directs our choice,
And we are led as we had sought,
" In word, in action, and in thought."

O soul that waitest still
      To hear the Voice Divine :
      As on the printed line
   Thou look'st to find God's will,
Look at thy life, and there find wrought
The blessing that thy lips have sought.

PRAISE.

Who praises thee as true man, praises Truth :
Pass that word on to *her*, ambitious youth !

PROVISION.

My thought goes o'er and o'er
To those who think no more—
Gone strangely out of sight,
And hushed in death's still night.

Loves still remain, but they
Who've left me on the way
Seem dearer since they've gone
Than these who still live on.

I know them better now;
Lives in the darkness show
Their whiteness best; and near,
One cannot see them clear.

Ah, if in that weird light
The vanished had their sight,
How would our lives appear
Who keep our dwelling here?

I cannot quite assent
To silent banishment—

To senseless, soulless rest;
Yet I would count that best,

Knew I that I might choose
My state;—I would refuse
A state on earth wherein
I might behold the sin

That smirches my beloved,
While to their sight I proved
But pure and true. God's love
Makes no such state above!

O friends long lost and still!
I cannot know your will
As once I knew; but I
Can leave you trustfully

In his great care who gave
The ground to hold your grave—
What I could do for you
Were poor when God doth do.

And if ye still have sense
Of his vast providence,

Or if ye senseless lie,
Ye're one with us, and I

Nor ye shall be alone,
Since God and we are one.
So, calm is in my heart,
And I would its peace impart,

When my thought goes o'er and o'er
To those who think no more—
Gone strangely out of sight,
And hushed in death's still night.

THE WAKENED HEART.

IN youth a matchless melody,
    That now I prize so dear,
Its answering chord found not in me,
    Its notes I could not hear.

But now I feel a joy complete
    The loving only know,
For day and night heaven's music sweet
    Beats on me here below.

TWO GROWTHS.

WHO lives a life of love outvies
 The soul that measures life by creed,
As roses in a garden rise
 Above the thriftless weed;

For loving souls, set in such ground
 They grow, and fruit and fragrance yield,
In more than King's array are crowned,
 Like lillies of the field.

THE KING'S DAUGHTER.

WHEN I was born, to me was given
Title to all in earth and heaven;
 My wealth's unspent;
Though Fortune's wheel go up or down,
It cannot rob me of my crown :
 I am content!

GRANT.

HE was not earth's commander—as we
    know.
  Some victories of great renown he gained;
  O'er mighty hosts he triumphed, and
    maintained,
Where others ran, the flag against the foe;
What, more than other mortals, could he
    show
  When Nature of her broken law com-
    plained?
  What slave so abject, soul and body
    chained,
When Evil Habit bade him come and go?

But when the King of Evil, Lord of Death,
  Began the siege against his purgèd soul,
  He found the great Commander in control,
And, with his utmost, could but take his breath!
So he who oft on earth was slain in strife
Hath won the grander fight 'twixt Death
    and Life.

A WORD TO O. W. H.

(On His Election as First Immortal.)

[FROM A DELEGATION OF HIS CONSTITUENTS.]

DEAR DR. HOLMES: Though we are late,
  We hope you'll let us through your portal,
For we would · fain congratulate
You on your quite exclusive fate
  Of standing as the First Immortal !

We hope ('tis all we've come to say,
  For though you've time enough to hear us,
As mortals long we cannot stay)—
With stories like "The One-Hoss Shay "
  We hope you'll never cease to cheer us;

And rhymes like those at college dinners,
  With tales of comet-ary visions,
And yarns, of which you're chief of spinners;
(For had we thought—we're selfish sinners—
  You'd drop your pen for "higher" missions,

We'd let you rattle on with those
  Who still, like us, are common mortals).
So still with witty verse and prose
Make light of mortals' fancied woes,
  Thou greatest of the Great Immortals!

.

LIVING WATERS.

WHEN I would drink an everlasting draught,
  I lock my doors to all the world's mixed
    drinks,
  Cease aught to care what any neighbor
    thinks,
And, all-alone as Adam when he quaffed

Eden's pure water, I drink in the thought
Of that great love which hath all beings
    wrought
With such desire for its own perfectness,
The more they drink, they yet desire no less.

INFLUENCE.

As Holy Spirit walks with each,
    And, silent as ourselves in thought,
    Moves us to do the things we ought
With tenfold force of angel's speech,
While rarely we the Power discern;
    So with us walk revered and loved,
    And, though nor tongue nor hand is
      moved,
Our minds they guide, our feet they turn,
And force that else we might have dared
    Impels to acts we dreamed not of.
    Who of his weakness needeth proof
May find it here. Who feels prepared
To stand alone against the world's loud scorn,
Should see that he from all mankind has torn.

MARY.

ALL the maids have died but one,—
  She will live forever;
In the Land of Love, the sun
  Setteth, fadeth never!

Maidens pure and lovers true
  Long the world has boasted,
But the maid that first we knew,
  Lover first we trusted—

Still the world holds none so dear;
  Nor to us shall any
(Though maids be for many a year,
  And lads be for many),

Dwell apart, star-souled and rare,
  While the fickle vary,
Like the maid that used to care
  For us with name of Mary.

HOPE.

THY heart, O God! is mine,
    Truest of all that love ;—
But mine's not wholly Thine,
    Or it would truer prove.

But since thy heart is mine,
    And Thou dost love for aye,
Mine shall be wholly thine
    When earth's loves fall away.

ON SEEING A BOY PLAYING CLAPPERS.

O GLEE! in a little boy's face,
    In his hands, in his feet, in his heart!
Should life set his soul such a race,
    That from hands and from feet thou de-
        part
    As they yield to Life s spiritless art,—
    O spirit, still stay in his heart!

CHRISTMAS MORNING.

WHAT other day from year to year
So fills the souls of men with cheer;
What memories are half so sweet
As those that in devotion meet,
    On Christmas morning?

The dawn upon the world's long night
Of him God sent to give it light
Hath spring of joy and blessedness
That faileth not nor groweth less,
    On Christmas morning.

I cannot hear the Christmas chimes,
Or list to Christmas singers' rhymes,
But tenderer my spirit grows,
And gladness all my speech o'erflows,
    On Christmas morning.

I cannot greet or young or old
But merry wishes manifold
Return to me; for like my own,
All hearts appear wide-open thrown
    On Christmas morning.

Our Christmas days on earth may be
How few God knoweth—only He;
Yet may our lives so Christlike grow
Each day our hearts shall feel the glow
    Of Christmas morning.

With Christmas cheer for all the year,—
A heart set free from care and fear,—
Our souls may ripe for Advent grow,
And thus each year more gladness know
    On Christmas morning.

MAN'S PART.

To eat and drink and build is all that the
    heavens decree :
For this were the worlds create, for this
    grows the land, flows the sea ;
And who eats and drinks and builds, like
    to God himself is he,—
And his is a part of the land, and his is a
    part of the sea.

THE DISCOVERY.

I KNOW, at last, why earth such beauty
    wears,
  Why hearts are tender, and hands reach to
    lift
The burdens that each says he, only, bears,
  When burden seems our solitary gift;

Why lives go on that fear had said would end;
  Why loves ford safely streams of sacrifice
Wherein who fell were lost; why bright
    hues blend
  When grief-storms pass; why even homes
    of vice

Are lit with sunbeams; and—oh, stranger
    yet!
  Why all this haps to thankless, cursing
    souls :
God, who made all—e'en these who him for-
    get—
  God's in the world, and still by love
    controls !